Exploring Stems

by Kristin Sterling

first step nonfiction

Lerner Publications Company · Minneapolis

I see **stems**.

Parts of a Plant

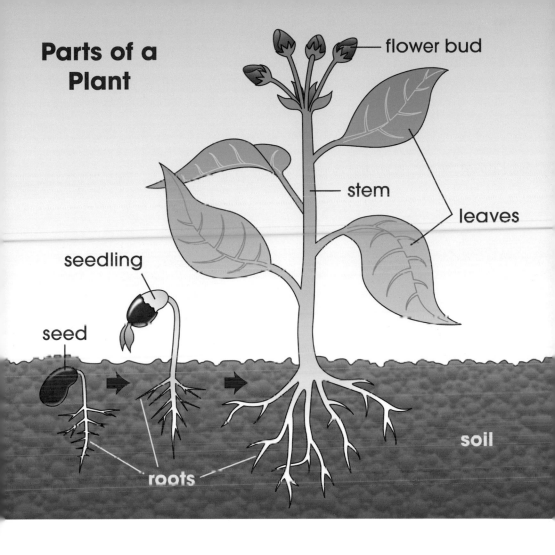

flower bud

stem

leaves

seedling

seed

roots

soil

Stems are parts of plants.

Plants need water, sunlight, and space to grow.

Stems help plants get the things they need.

Stems grow above the soil.

They **connect** to roots
below the soil.

Stems act like straws.

They carry water to leaves
and flowers.

Stems hold up plants.

They help leaves get
sunlight and air.

Tree trunks are stems.

These stems are covered with bark.

People eat some kinds of stems. Celery is a tasty stem.

Panda bears eat the stems
of bamboo grass.

Stems are on your plate, in the park, and all around you.

Do you see stems?

Stems We Eat

asparagus

rhubarb

celery

sugarcane

Stem Facts

 People use stems for many reasons. Wood from tree trunks is used to make paper and to build houses.

 Stems can be stiff or bendable. Tree trunks are stiff. Daisy stems bend.

 Some plants have climbing stems. Ivy stems can grow up the sides of houses.

 Sugar in candy comes from the stems of sugarcane plants.

Pancake syrup comes from sap in the trunks of maple trees. People make a hole and let the sap drip into buckets.

 Some stems have thorns to keep animals away. Lemon trees have thorns.

 Most desert plants store water in their stems, roots, and leaves.

Glossary

 connect – to join together

 roots – parts of a plant that bring in water and keep a plant in the ground

 soil – the dirt in which plants grow

 stems – the parts of a plant that hold up the plant

Index

The images in this book are used with the permission of: © Steve Satushek/Botanica/Getty Images, pp. 2, 22 (bottom); © Laura Westlund/Independent Picture Service, p. 3; © Eastcott Momatiuk/The Image Bank/Getty Images, p. 4; © Raulin/Dreamstime.com, p. 5; © Rob D. Casey/Botanica/Getty Images, p. 6; © Scott Sinklier/AGStockUSA/Alamy, pp. 7, 22 (top), (second from top), (third from top); © JGI/Jamie Grill/Blend Images/Getty Images, p. 8; © Nick Servian/Alamý, p. 9; © iStockphoto.com/Graeme Nicholson, p. 10; © Sami Sarkis RM CC/Alamy, p. 11; © joSon/Taxi/Getty Images, p. 12; © Randy Olson/National Geographic/Getty Images, p. 13; © Jupiterimages/Comstock Images/Getty Images, p. 14; © Hotshotsworldwide/Dreamstime.com, p. 15; © Compassionate Eye Foundation/Drew Kelly/Digital Vision/Getty Images, p. 16; © Aerogondo/Dreamstime.com, p. 17; © iStockphoto.com/Diane Diederich, p. 18 (left); © Daseaford/Dreamstime.com, p. 18 (right); © iStockphoto.com/Alfredo Maiquez, p. 19 (left); © Clive Chilvers/Dreamstime.com, p. 19 (right). Front Cover: © Asiavasmuncky/Dreamstime.com.

Main body text set in ITC Avant Garde Gothic 21/25. Typeface provided by Adobe Systems.

Lerner Publications Company
A division of Lerner Publishing Group, Inc.
241 First Avenue North
Minneapolis, MN 55401 U.S.A.

Website address: www.lernerbooks.com

Library of Congress Cataloging-in-Publication Data

Sterling, Kristin.
    Exploring stems / by Kristin Sterling.
        p.   cm. — (First step nonfiction — Let's look at plants)
    Includes index.
    ISBN: 978-0-7613-5783-4 (lib. bdg. : alk. paper)
    1. Stems (Botany)—Juvenile literature. 2. Plant anatomy—Juvenile literature. I. Title.
    II. Series: First step nonfiction. Plant parts.
    QK646.S74 2012
    581.4'95—dc22   2010042991

Manufactured in the United States of America
1 – PC – 7/15/11